Chicago Bee Branch
3647 S. State Street
Chicago, IL 60609

George Eastman
The Kodak Camera Man

Carin T. Ford

Enslow Publishers, Inc.

40 Industrial Road   PO Box 38
Box 398   Aldershot
Berkeley Heights, NJ 07922   Hants GU12 6BP
USA   UK
http://www.enslow.com

Library of Congress Cataloging-in-Publication Data

Ford, Carin T.
George Eastman : the Kodak camera man / Carin T. Ford.
    p. cm. — (Famous inventors)
Summary: Describes the life and career of the man who revolutionized photography by developing a camera simple enough for anyone to use.
ISBN 0-7660-2247-1
1. Eastman, George, 1854–1932—Juvenile literature. 2. Photographic industry—United States—Biography—Juvenile literature. [1. Eastman, George, 1854–1932. 2. Inventors. 3. Photography—History.] I. Title. II. Series.
TR140.E3F67   2003
770'.92—dc21

                                                                    2003006480

Printed in the United States of America

10 9 8 7 6 5 4 3 2 1

To Our Readers: We have done our best to make sure all Internet Addresses in this book were active and appropriate when we went to press. However, the author and the publisher have no control over and assume no liability for the material available on those Internet sites or on other Web sites they may link to. Any comments or suggestions can be sent by e-mail to comments@enslow.com or to the address on the back cover.

Every effort has been made to locate all copyright holders of material used in this book. If any errors or omissions have occurred, corrections will be made in future editions of this book.

Kodak is a registered Trademark of Eastman Kodak Company.

Illustration Credits: Courtesy George Eastman House, pp. 10–11, 13, 14, 17, 19, 22T, 25; Reproduced from the Dictionary of American Portraits, Published by Dover Publications, Inc., in 1967, p. 4 (portrait); From the Collections of Henry Ford Museum & Greenfield Village, p. 22B; Library of Congress, pp. 3, 4 (inset), 6, 8, 12, 16; National Archives, p. 28; © Rachel Shopiro Studios, pp. 7, 20, 24, 26, 27; © Rachel Shopiro Studios, Photo by Julian Alexander, pp. 1, 2; Rebecca Weber, p. 21.

Cover Illustration: Portrait, Courtesy George Eastman House. Box camera, © Rachel Shopiro Studios. Brownie camera, © Rachel Shopiro Studios, Photo by Julian Alexander. Folding Kodak camera, Rebecca Weber.

Table of Contents

1 Hard Work 5

2 New Ideas 9

3 In Business 15

4 The Kodak Camera 18

5 Changing the World 23

Timeline. 29

Words to Know 30

Learn More About George Eastman 31
    (Books and Internet Addresses)

Index 32

Old cameras were too big and heavy to hold. George Eastman decided to change that.

Chapter 1

Hard Work

George Eastman was planning a trip. The year was 1877, and George was twenty-three years old. His friend had an idea: George should buy a camera and take pictures of his vacation. Back then, very few people had cameras. Most cameras were owned by photographers who took pictures for a living.

George bought a camera and the other things he would need. Altogether, everything weighed almost

This is the first picture ever taken of George.

fifty pounds. Then he paid for lessons on how to use it. Soon, George forgot all about going on his trip. There was only one thing he wanted to do—take pictures.

George would spend the rest of his life taking pictures and inventing cameras that were smaller and easier to use.

George was born on July 12, 1854, in Waterville, New York. He had two older sisters: Ellen Maria, age nine, and Emma Kate, four. Their parents were George and Maria Eastman. In 1860, the family moved to Rochester, New York. There, his father ran a school to teach people the skills they would need to work in an office.

George was only seven years old when his father died. To earn money, George's mother took in boarders. These were people who paid to eat and sleep in the Eastmans' house. By the time George was fourteen, he decided to quit school and find a job. He wanted to help his family. He worked every day except Sunday, from 8 A.M. to 6 P.M., sweeping floors and running errands.

In a notebook, George listed all the money he earned and all the money he spent. He gave some of his money to his mother. With the rest, he paid for haircuts, clothing, dancing lessons, and vacations. After a year, he changed jobs to earn even more.

George was born in this house.

George was no longer in school, but he did not stop learning. George knew he needed a good education. He often stood in a bookstore, reading for hours. He took lessons in French. He borrowed books from the library. He took classes to learn skills that he would need to run a business.

George Eastman was a hard worker all his life.

George lived most of his life in Rochester, New York. This photo shows the city in 1888.

Chapter 2

New Ideas

When George was nineteen, he took a job at a bank. Within two years, he was earning enough to pay all his bills. George moved with his mother to a nicer house. He enjoyed going out to concerts and plays.

George liked music, and he wanted to play the flute. He practiced and practiced—but he did not sound very good. Then he found a new interest: photography.

Taking pictures was wonderful! There was so much to learn. The first camera George bought, at age twenty-three, was a big box. It did not use film, like many cameras today. Instead, the picture was recorded on a large glass plate. Each glass plate took one picture.

First, George had to smear the plate with wet chemicals. Then he placed it inside his camera. The camera was too heavy to hold, so he put it on a three-legged stand called a tripod. After taking a picture, George quickly carried the glass plate into a dark tent. Before the plate dried, he had to treat it

with more chemicals to bring out the picture. Making just one picture took almost an hour.

George began to look for an easier way to take

In this early camera, each photo was taken on a wet glass plate.

glass plate

chemicals

tripod

pictures. He read everything he could find on the subject. George learned that some photographers in England were using dry plates instead of wet ones. It was simpler and faster. George liked this idea. He wanted to come up with his own way of making dry-plate pictures.

George worked all day at the bank and all night on his experiments with dry plates. He turned his mother's kitchen into a laboratory. He cooked chemical recipes on the stove and baked them on glass plates in the oven. Many nights, George fell asleep in his clothes on the kitchen floor.

George had been working with cameras for a little more than two years. At last he came up with a dry plate that worked. Next, he

George worked in a bank like this one.

This is the first picture that George ever took.
It shows the Genesee River in Rochester.

invented a machine that spread a thin coat of the chemical mixture onto the glass plates.

In 1880, George rented a room in an office building. Here he made more dry plates. He still worked at the bank, too. Every day, George rode to the bank on his bicycle. His lunch was tied on the back in a shoe box. At three o'clock, he left the bank and biked to his workshop. There he made dry plates all night long. Sometimes he stopped for a nap.

George's new company sold dry plates.

All of George's hard work paid off. Many photographers began to buy his dry plates. With his business making money, he could quit his job at the bank. On January 1, 1881, George opened the Eastman Dry Plate Company.

Chapter 3

In Business

S oon after George started his business, it faced a big problem. He had been selling hundreds of dry plates a month. Suddenly, photographers said the plates were not working. Most of the pictures were not coming out at all. The others were very foggy.

George did more than 450 experiments before he figured out what was wrong. A chemical was missing from the mixture that coated the plates. He took back all the bad dry plates he had sold. He replaced them with good ones. This cost the Eastman Dry Plate Company a lot of money. But George did not give up. Because he was so honest, people felt they could trust his company. The business continued to grow.

George was always thinking of new ideas.

Then George had another idea. His dry plates made photography easier, but most people did not own a camera. At that time, cameras were still too heavy and difficult to use.

George decided he would come up with a new kind of camera. He said he would make it as easy to use as a pencil.

George's factory building in Rochester in 1881.

Chapter 4

The Kodak Camera

George knew that first he had to get rid of the glass plates. Instead, George wanted to use paper to take pictures. He hired William H. Walker to help him. Together, they experimented with spreading chemicals on sheets of paper. The paper was cut into strips and wrapped around a spool. This was put into a roll holder that fit into people's cameras. As the paper rolled from one spool to another one, it could take many pictures. George called his invention "American film."

George thought that photographers would be happy to buy his film instead of heavy glass plates. But he was wrong. So how could his company make money selling film? George had to get cameras into the hands of more people. He decided to make a smaller, cheaper camera that used film.

George invented some film. Then he used it to take this picture of himself. He wrote a few notes on the photo.

When George was thirty-two years old, he invented a new camera. For the next two years, he worked hard to make sure it was easy to use and took clear pictures. By 1888, George was ready to sell his camera. It was about four inches wide and seven inches long. It came loaded with film for one hundred pictures. Weighing just over a pound, this camera

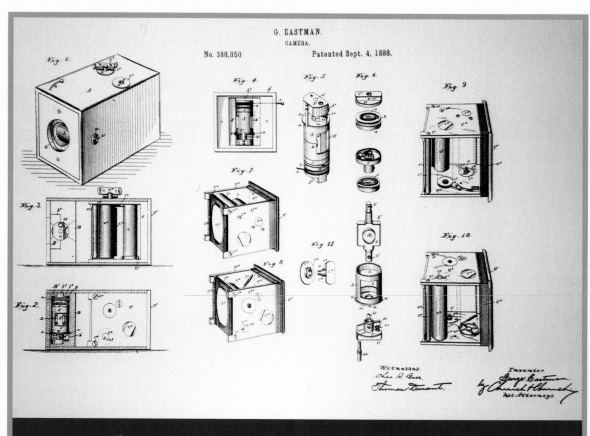

These drawings show the different parts of George's first Kodak camera.

was so light that no tripod was needed to hold it. To take a picture, all a person had to do was pull a string to open the camera's "eye," turn a key to wind the film, aim, and press the button.

Once all the film was used up, the whole camera was mailed back to George's company. There, the film was taken out of the camera in a darkroom, and the pictures were developed. Then the camera was loaded with more film and sent back along with the pictures.

Some Kodak cameras could be folded up. This made them easy to carry.

Now all George needed was a name for his camera. He wanted something that people

Open   Closed

The photographs taken by the Kodak camera were round.

would remember. George liked the letter "K" because it sounded strong. So he made up a new word. He called his camera "Kodak."

The Kodak camera was a big success. Suddenly, everyone was excited about taking pictures. Photography became the new American hobby.

George's new camera was so simple to use!

THE KODAK CAMERA.

"You press the button, -
- - - we do the rest."

The only camera that anybody can use without instructions. Send for the Primer, free.

The Kodak is for sale by all Photo stock dealers.

The Eastman Dry Plate and Film Co.,

Price $25.00—Loaded for 100 Pictures.   ROCHESTER, N. Y.

A full line Eastman's goods always in stock at LOEBER BROS,, 111 Nassau Street, New York.

Chapter 5

Changing the World

Georgé Eastman was very busy. By 1889, his company was developing film from 700 cameras every day. George built factories in New York, London, and Paris.

In 1891, George's company came out with "daylight-loading" film. This was packed in a special holder that kept the film in darkness. People could put this film into their cameras all by themselves.

Children loved George's Kodak Brownie camera.

They did not need their own darkroom.

George now called his business the Eastman Company. In 1892, he changed the name to the Eastman Kodak Company. George kept inventing new kinds of cameras. Each one was smaller and easier to use. At his factories, George was known as a very good boss. He treated his workers well.

Even though George had become very rich, he never forgot what it was like to be poor. He wanted to make a camera that anyone could buy. In 1900, George created his most famous camera of all, called the Brownie. It cost only $1 and took small, square pictures. Because it was so easy to use, it was very popular with children.

George had always believed that education is very

important. Back when he had earned only $60 a week, he had given $50 to a school, the Mechanics Institute, now called the Rochester Institute of Technology. Now that he had millions of dollars, George gave away huge amounts of money to other colleges and hospitals. He also set up dental clinics around the world so that poor children could have healthy teeth.

George liked using his money to help others. On one

Everyone was amazed to see such a small camera.

day in 1924, he gave a total of $30 million to three colleges. "Now I feel better," he said. Often, George would use the name "Mr. Smith" when he gave away large sums of money. He did not want a lot of attention. Even though George was famous around the world, he was still a shy man.

When he became rich, George built his dream house.

George never married. He lived in a large house with fifty rooms. He invited people over every Sunday night. George filled his home with fresh flowers and asked musicians to play for his guests.

George liked to hear music all around him, but he did not want to see where it came from. He kept the organ hidden behind lots of plants.

George enjoyed all kinds of music. He had a pipe organ in his house and his own organist. When George came downstairs every morning at 7:30, his organist would begin to play. George listened to this music every day as he ate breakfast and dinner.

George also liked to travel. He took many trips and even went on two safaris in Africa. George always had a camera with him, and he took pictures of elephants, zebras, and rhinos.

When Thomas Edison, right, developed a movie camera, he used some of George's film.

George was especially happy at his country house in North Carolina. There, he liked to go horseback riding and fishing. He hunted quail and wild turkeys. He had built a music school nearby, and sometimes he invited the schoolchildren to come to his house and sing.

George died on March 14, 1932. He was seventy-seven years old. George Eastman was a hardworking man who shared his riches to help other people. His invention of the Kodak camera turned photography into a hobby that everyone could enjoy.

Timeline

1854~George Eastman is born in Waterville, New York, on July 12.

1862~His father dies.

1868~Quits school to get a job.

1877~Buys his first camera and learns to use it.

1880~Begins selling dry plates to photographers.

1881~Starts the Eastman Dry Plate Company.

1884~Invents paper "American film."

1888~Creates a small box camera and calls it "Kodak."

1900~Introduces the Kodak Brownie camera, selling for $1.

1932~Dies on March 14 in Rochester, New York.

Words to Know

chemical—A liquid, solid, or gas that can cause a change in something else.

darkroom—A very dark place for developing film into pictures.

develop—Using chemicals to bring out the pictures on glass plates or film.

film—A thin material that is coated with chemicals to make photographs.

glass plates—Plates coated with chemicals that were used to make photographs before film was invented.

hobby—Something a person does for fun.

photography—Making photographs with a camera.

photographer—A person who takes pictures for fun or as a job.

safari—A hunting trip, especially in Africa.

Learn More

Books

Gibbons, Gail. *Click! A Book About Cameras and Taking Pictures*. New York: Little, Brown & Co., 1997.

Joseph, Paul. *George Eastman*. Minneapolis, Minn.: Abdo & Daughters, 1997.

Mitchell, Barbara. *Click! A Story About George Eastman*. Minneapolis, Minn.: Lerner Publishing Group, 1986.

Internet Addresses

History of Kodak. <http://www.kodak.com/US/en/corp/aboutKodak/kodakHistory/kodakHistory.shtml>

PBS/WGBH. "The Wizard of Photography." The American Experience, 1999. <http://www.pbs.org/wgbh/amex/eastman>

Index

D

daylight-loading
  film, 23
dry plates, 12, 14,
  15–16

E

early cameras,
  10–12
Eastman Dry Plate
  Company, 14, 16
Eastman, Ellen
  Maria (sister), 6
Eastman, Emma
  Kate (sister), 6
Eastman, George
  birth, 6
  childhood, 6–8
  death, 28
  donations, 25–26
  early interest in
    cameras, 5–6,
    9–12

education, 7, 8
hobbies, 9, 27,
  28
jobs, 7, 9, 12, 14
love of music, 9,
  27, 28
Eastman, George
  (father), 6
Eastman Kodak
  Company, 24
Eastman, Maria
  (mother), 6, 7, 9,
  12
Edison, Thomas,
  28

G

glass plates, 10,
  12, 14, 18, 19

K

Kodak Brownie,
  24

Kodak camera,
  first, 19–22

M

Mechanics
  Institute, 25

P

paper film, 18–19

R

Rochester
  Institute of
  Technology, 25
Rochester,
  New York, 6, 8

W

Walker,
  William H., 18
Waterville,
  New York, 6
wet plates, 10–12